Self-Discipline Unlimited

7 Easy Steps to Unlock Your Best Habits

By L.J. Axon

author is not engaging in the rendering of legal, financial, medical, or professional advice. The content within this book has been derived from various sources. Please consult a licensed professional before attempting any techniques outlined in this book.

By reading this document, the reader agrees that under no circumstances is the author responsible for any losses, direct or indirect, that are incurred as a result of the use of information contained within this document, including, but not limited to, errors, omissions, or inaccuracies.

Table of Contents

Step Seven: Taking Action

Conclusion

Introduction

I find it odd how people largely think of habits as being associated with our vices or bad behavior. Of course, we all have habits attributed to poor behavior, such as smoking or biting your nails, but do habits have to retain a negative connotation? Have you ever asked yourself how is a habit formed? What is the difference between a habit and normal, human behavior? How can you increase your good habits?

When you start to understand how the brain works, you will also understand how to manipulate it into performing better. Therefore, this book will not only give you a list of things you can do to attain it but explains how the mind works in relation to positive, habit forming behavior. It will also explore what seven steps you need to take to make a difference in the way that you live your life. Did you know, for example, that the habits you have can be overwritten?

The reason I wrote this book is because I understand how hard it is to keep up with every aspect of our busy lives, and I wanted to try and help people address that. I also believe that a lot of people do not live up to their full potential because they are unable to see the outcome through the effort it takes to achieve it. There is so much distraction in this world that we often forget many of the things that are profoundly important. Do you know what self-discipline really is? If the answer is no, then I hope you will find the answer within the pages of this book. The steps that I mention here will help you to move toward a better life.

They do so by showing you the means of changing your habits to improve your overall approach to life.

I have taken an approach that covers all areas of our lives. For example, if you need positivity in your life, the steps that you take toward the achievement of self-discipline will help you to experience that positivity. Toward the end of this book, in the last chapter, you will discover habits that successful people practice. My aim in helping you discover this is to help you bring all of your progress together, using the different methods demonstrated throughout the book.

I genuinely hope that this book makes a difference in your life. I have written it as an easy to understand and easy to read book to be absorbed at your leisure. I did not see much point in producing a highly scientific book that people get bored with after the first pages. This is a text that hits hard with facts, principles and ideals, and can be referenced over and over again. It takes a human approach, and one that will set you on the right course to help you unlock both habits and skills alike.

Chapter One: What is Self-Discipline?

"Hold yourself responsible for a higher standard than anybody else expects of you. Never excuse yourself. Never pity yourself. Be a hard master to yourself-and be lenient to everybody else." - **Henry Ward Beecher**

After reading the above quotation, some may feel the advice it holds somewhat challenging. The only person you can be responsible for in this life is you. The expectations that you have of yourself will dictate your level of self-discipline. The one thing you should bear in mind is that although you should expect the best of yourself, that does not mean being a perfectionist. Far from it. It means knowing your own capabilities, improving upon those capabilities, and taking responsibility for your own actions. It does not mean measuring yourself against others. When you try to do that, you almost always find you will come up short. That is when biases set in, which increases the chances of you abandoning your task. You need to be aware of the raw material that you are working with, i.e., your mind, and look at your own capabilities and take every opportunity to improve them as and when you can.

Self-discipline also means confronting your responsibilities, without blame or regret. It is all about YOU and the way that you face problems and deal with them. If you typically put things off because they are too tedious or require more of you than you are willing to give, then you are not using self-discipline to its fullest potential. However, it does not have to be as hard to comprehend as that. There are certain levels of energy in everyone that fluctuate over the course of a day, and it is up to you to identify when they are at their best. Sufficient rest and sleep will ensure that you have high levels of energy in the morning. After you have eaten a light lunch, the break that you give yourself away from work should energize you for the early part of the afternoon. These are periods when you can use self-discipline to complete important tasks that require a little more brainwork. When self-discipline is active, you find that not only will you do the things you need to do, but usually better manage your time so you can enjoy life as well. It is not just about work; it is also about balance.

So, what inspires self-discipline in one person and fails another?

Let us now explore some of the things that impede self-discipline. These are good starting points to help understand the overall concept. The following traits will almost certainly inhibit the growth of self-discipline in you.

| You have no goals | If you do not have goals, you cannot measure your progress. |
| You put things off | This is a mild form of procrastination but if you do it often enough and it can turn into a habit that is difficult to |

	eradicate.
You are overwhelmed	You have not put any order into the things you have to do but view them as one entity.
You feel others do not put in enough effort	This is self-evasion. It is not about others; it is about you.
You have developed lazy habits	I will explain later in the book about habit formation and explain how you can overwrite them.
You do not prioritize	Therefore, you never know which things are of the utmost urgency.
You are afraid of criticism and failure	These fears are unfounded once you understand that failure provides opportunity. Explained in more detail later on.
You do not agree you require guidance on self-discipline.	Then I'm glad you are here!

From the above examples, you observe that self-discipline is something you impose on yourself. It is nothing to do with the expectations of others. Some may blame their boss, their family, etc. but your life has taken you to this point. Because you have chosen the job you have, you have a personal responsibility to do that job. Because you are lucky enough to have the family you have, you also have a personal responsibility to live within the structure of a family. Everything boils down to your choices, your habits, and your way of dealing with life. It does not have to be as hard as many make it out to be and, over the course of the next few chapters, I will show you why.

You will also learn how to change some of your habits so that you are able to do more; even if you feel you are working at your maximum capacity right now. To maximize what you will learn in this book you need to understand the workings of your own body and mind to be able to make changes to the way you operate. Therefore, please bear with me while we briefly explore the biological function of the brain. I have included this information in the book to help you to grasp a better understanding of habits and how they are formed. Over the course of these upcoming chapters, you will be taught to exercise self-discipline and learn how to change your habits for the better. Therefore, the next chapter deals with habits and habit formation.

Chapter Two: Habits and How They are Formed

"Depending on what they are, our habits will either make us or break us. We become what we repeatedly do." - **Sean Covey**

I want you to read the quote at the beginning of this chapter again. The keywords mentioned explain that we are responsible for our own level of success, and that what we do on a regular basis defines who we are. Let me give you an example. There are some habits in your life that you follow without consideration, primarily because of the way that your brain is mapped. You have millions of thoughts in a single day, a certain amount of which will be negative because of our inherent predispositions. Many of these are vestiges of our hunter-gatherer past. It was an imperative thought process due to the increased dangers of the time-period and the need to survive.

Now, contemplate what happens to all those thoughts. For example, the writer who forgets to write down a clever line that came to them will ultimately forget it and may never recall it again. The reason? It is not a habit; it is a thought. A more personal example would be your morning routine. You clean your teeth every morning, drive your car without even really having to physically think about where the gear shift is or what you need to do when you arrive at an intersection. Generally, you start your day in automatic mode. Why? Well, the things that you do are repeatedly being registered as important to you. These thoughts reside in the part of the brain that deals with long term memories. You know when to change gear. You know when you want your next glass of water. It happens because the part of your brain that stores this information is quicker to action than the conscious mind. You do not think about these things before you do them. You just do them. If you had to think with your conscious mind of every action, it would slow you down considerably. However, because of your long-term memory function, it is unnecessary.

This kind of information tells us that if you can form a habit by repeating a pattern you can replace that habit and use it to help create and develop self-discipline. If you repeat an action time and time again, studies have shown that after about 4 to 5 weeks, you will find that the action becomes part of your day with little conscious thought attached. Let me give you an example. Supposing that you are not particularly motivated when it comes to keeping fit. You wake up in the morning and instead of getting out of bed and going for a run, you turn the alarm off and go back to sleep. If you force yourself to have that run, after 5 weeks or so, you will no longer attribute conscious thought to it. It will become just another part of your automatic life routine.

Step One: Understanding your Existing Habits

But how can you relate and apply this to other habits? By another method called habit stacking. To help improve its success, I use the 'piggybacking' method. So, for step one, I want you to identify and understand your existing habits. The reason being is because until you do, you will not understand which of these habits is a bad habit or a good habit. There will also be habits you may fail to recognize because you have never consciously looked for them. I have a suggestion. Keep a notepad on you for the next week or so and write down all the things you do that you consider being habits. Not just things you think are habits, but those things you perform in an automatic, habit-like manner. As an example, let us look at what this can look like in written form.

I always laugh when I am uncomfortable
I always go to the toilet in the morning
I always clean my teeth after I wash my face
I always leave my shoes in the front hall instead of the shoe cupboard
I always play with my fingernails when I am talking
I always play with my hair when I am impatient

Some of these things you may already do, maybe your list does not include any of these behaviors at all. It is important that next to each habit you markdown you to leave sufficient space underneath it for Step Two. The reason for this will become clear in the next chapter. What you are trying to do is get familiar with your habits and, in turn, increasingly familiar with yourself. If you do something by impulse and do it on a regular basis, it is a habit. I rub my hands together when I am nervous. I noticed this when I was observing my own habits. Similarly, you will have things you do that you fail to observe as normal practice. I want you to be as open and honest as possible going forward because it is paramount for your progress.

Your self-discipline, and the improvement of it, depends upon keen self-observation. The reason? Because much of what you do can be fitted into habits, and once they are, they no longer demotivate your self-discipline. It takes nominal effort to sustain, and one of its greatest benefits is the productivity it affords you. Consistent results then become the ultimate motivator. They also serve as proof that the self-discipline aspect of the process helps you succeed in life through the habits that you acquire intentionally.

There may be habits you find difficult to deal with; it is entirely expected when on any journey to self-development. With that in mind, over the course of this book I will show you how self-discipline comes into play and how the implementation of small changes can help you to adjust your perspective. Once you have listed and begun to understand your habits over the course of the next week, you will be able to decide which habits are reasonable and which need to be replaced. The goal here is to help you maximize your good habits and minimize the bad ones. I'm not saying that I expect you to drop all of your bad habits overnight. You have acquired these habits over an incredibly long period of time, so you will need to reinvest time in yourself to facilitate their change and evolution.

The other aspect that you need to look it is why these habits formed. You must try your best to understand them and associate with the reasons. This will help you to see why you initially embraced the habit, and why you believe this habit is of benefit in your life.

The other aspect is to look at the habit of negative thoughts and assess why you sometimes do not perform to your full potential. This is where the principle of self-discipline will be of great benefit. When you decide upon a mental trait you would like to work on, and understand its origin, you can then utilize the principles of self-discipline to help eliminate thoughts that present the greatest resistance. These are mental processes you must believe in, commit to, and repeat on a regular basis. One of the natural enemies of this type of thinking is the ability your brain possesses to store negative thoughts as positive ones. You have repeated this process on a regular basis throughout your life because your mind naturally sees these behaviors as being important to you. If they were not important to you, then you would not repeat them.

I do not like new things	Work out why you do not like new things. Just because you failed in the past, does not mean you will continue to fail.

I am not highly thought of	What event in the past made you believe this?
I am not adventurous	Again, what made you believe this?
I can never catch a break	Examine your thoughts and work out why you think this
I will never be successful	Why would anyone believe that?
I do not have what it takes	Again, what makes you believe that?

The point of this exercise is to show you that the habit of negative thinking about your own abilities is what limits your improvement rather than an actual lack of abilities. None of the above statements are true, unless you think they are. Therefore, the solution lies in the way in which you look at your life. Many of the concepts people believe ring true about their lives derive from childhood experiences or comments. Childhood is a highly impressionable time in our lives, and if we become accustom to hearing and believing something is true, it becomes so. If we are not given positive affirmation as a child, we carry that with us into our adult life. These are the type of habits we must attempt to rewrite. The only way you can undertake such a task is by identifying and understanding them, then working on positive affirmation to reinforce your objective.

The next time you catch yourself thinking negatively about you and your situation make it a habit of replacing the thought by rephrasing it in a positive way. "I can't" turns into "I can always try new things," or "I cannot afford it," turns into "How can I afford it?" If you practice doing this every time that the negative thought comes to your mind, the thought will eventually be replaced. Similarly, you can change "I am useless" into "I have my uses" as does everyone. The self-discipline is held in being accountable for your own actions and thoughts because we can become what we believe we are. We are not any less valuable than others unless we believe it to be the case. Often, we use these excuses in our lives to avoid trying new things. However, new achievements will almost always make you feel good about yourself.

Try small things that you have never tried before. Bake a cake, read a book, or do a puzzle. Whatever it is that you choose to do, do it to the best of your ability and reward yourself for completing it. We all have negativity within us, and the human mind reverts to negative thinking on regular occasions. As discussed, the mind once used negativity for survival when mankind depended upon aspects such as reflexes and compliance for survival. Of course, we still need to exercise vigilance in our lives, but negativity must not be used as the principle guide in our lives.

Therefore, you must explore your habits and discover which generate feelings of value and which do not. You can eliminate some of the negative elements in your life using self-discipline. If you are a procrastinator, start to do things instead of thinking about doing them. Once practiced, you learn to adopt and welcome the beginning of any process and greet new challenges with open arms. Remember, if you consistently tell yourself that you cannot complete a task, you are limiting your own potential growth as a human being.

Remember to come armed with the list of your daily habits for the next chapter of the book. You will need it, because this is where you will be able to use those habits to your advantage. The purpose of the next chapter is to really examine your habits. We will then explore the possibility of replacing bad habits in favor of something more positive. About thoughts, we will discover how accessible habit-forming is using affirmation instead of habitual negative thought. If you practice positive habit-forming enough and motivate your mind not to accept a negative outcome, your self-discipline will work in your favor. Of course, not all habits are so easy to break. But, when you exercise self-discipline as a habit, you will also enable growth in other areas of your life.

Chapter Three: Leapfrogging

Step Two: Leapfrogging Habits

Now, let us examine list of habits that you have. Ignore the bad ones for now, just think about habits that would be beneficial to you. For example, creating a to-do list the night before helps you organize tasks that you have for tomorrow. A list gives you a true picture of what you need to achieve the next day and becomes a mental motivator that will provide a clear path to follow. When creating your list, make sure you start out by writing down two or three tasks only. A short-term spike of multiple rapid actions will only produce short-term results. Taking on too much too soon can be counter productive and demotivating, especially if you consistently fail to achieve everything on your list. You must practice long-term actions to produce long-term solutions. Therefore, it is far better at this stage to make yourself a list that you will be able to comply with. Crossing out items on your list will give you a positive feeling of accomplishment that will keep you motivated and will boost your self-esteem.

What do you normally do at bedtime as a habit? If you shower and then get into bed, what do you do immediately once in bed? If you read, could you replace five minutes of that reading with the habit of creating your to-do list? Or read then before you go to sleep, work out your to-do list for tomorrow? The idea behind this is to complete your task-list in advance so that when you wake, you know exactly what needs to be done and can start to achieve it.

Introducing additional habits to your current list of daily habits makes the process easier. For example, when you are finished in the shower, tidy up. When you finish your breakfast, place the dishes in the dishwasher. Once you have arrived at work, park a little further away than normal and walk the rest of the way.

During this process keep in mind that every time that you introduce a new habit, it can take up to 40 days to work its way into your subconscious. You will find it a difficult undertaking in the beginning, as with all new endeavors, but as you gradually add it to your subconscious mind you will find yourself doing each task automatically.

I wish more people acknowledged and utilized leapfrogging. It has such a positive effect on the whole process of building effective habits. Used successfully, you can use the technique to create more time in your day. Let me tell you about a habit that changed my life for the better. I used to find that housework was a bane to say the least. It was something I did not really want to spend my weekends doing, because I was so busy during the rest of my week. Eating into my free time was not something that appealed.

So, I introduced a new habit into my life that allowed me to stay tidy with minimal effort. Every time that any person within my household left a room, I politely asked that they took something with them. It was a small habit, but when I multiplied that by the number of people in my house, I found that by the weekend, I had hardly anything to tidy because it had already been done. I even convinced my children to form the habit by turning into a game and/or competition. They complied.

When you catch your five-year-old trying to straighten a picture in the living room because it is the only thing out of place, it is a truly marvelous experience.

Why does habit stacking work?

Because you are using established habits to create new ones. You already habit stack in your life and may not even be aware of it. For example, when you learned to drive going for a short drive required substantial mental effort. You were unsure of the width of your vehicle. You were unsure of your own personal skills as a driver, so you had to be acutely aware and conscious of every action. Now, when you get into your car, it is completely different. You understand what to do. Putting the key in the ignition follows the habit of getting into the car automatically. The actions you follow while you are driving have become automated. You look in the mirror, followed by signaling. You turn while making yourself aware of any obstacles present. You change lanes effortlessly. You turn on the radio or even answer your hand's free telephone without having to think about it. Why? Because each of these habits has been tagged onto one that already exists.

The same goes for the way that you treat your workplace. If you get into the habit of managing distractions to prioritize tasks at the beginning of the day, then you will find your habits will decrease outside interference. After that, you have an existing habit of going to the coffee machine. Add another habit – How about going outside for a few minutes to get some fresh air? The reason habit stacking works is because you have existing habits and timelines that you perform daily. All you are doing is extending and adding to them, which requires far less effort than attempting to establish a new habit without a timescale.

Chapter Four: Why You Need to Prioritize

"Focus on being productive, instead of busy" - **Tim Ferris**

If you break down our high and low energy segments over the course of a day, it looks like this:

Your high energy levels make up 50% and occur usually early morning or right after lunch.

Your medium energy makes up approx. 25%.

Your winding-down energy about 20%.

Your leisure and sport energy make up 5%.

The important thing to realize and understand here is that you need to manage your time, so you are undertaking all high priority tasks within your high-energy time. This will provide you with the most energy available to you to deal with them effectively. These tasks are prioritized as in need of immediate attention. Your medium energy phase occurs just before lunch and in the late afternoon. There are many low-energy tasks that can be undertake during this time with minimal effort. The idea is to create the following habit:

Step Three: Prioritize What You Have to Do

Saying that, your winding down energy is just as important and can also be used to good effect. For example, this energy can help you get a good night's sleep or generate new ideas. Using your leisure energy effectively usually denotes taking part in some form of physical exercise. The absolute minimum for leisure time is shown on the chart, and you need to find something you can do that expends that energy in an effective and interesting or fun way. It may be a trip to the gym, a walk with the dog, or even cycling. One of the less often considerations of physical exercise is that energy creates energy. Hence, when you are physically fitter and more energy, you increase your productivity.

One of the other aspects you need to focus on is how you can eat healthier during the working day. This can be of great benefit because if you snack often, it can increase your chances of health problems large or small. If you snack at work, or eat your lunch in a rush, you are not giving your body the correct amount of time it needs to digest the food. Health must always come first, especially when you are trying to become more productive, so prioritizing your responsibilities will only help to get your life into order sooner. As a positive byproduct of this method it will also help, and inspire, you to create increased self-discipline. You are the only one responsible for your body, your health, and your wellbeing. So, when you begin to apply effective time management to habits you are trying to build, you naturally create increased positive habits.

So, what do priorities usually consist of?

• Work that must be completed

• Work that appears less urgent to complete

• Work that appears routine

• Work you can effectively delegate

You must prioritize your most urgent work and manage all interruptions so that you can work to an effective timetable. This means concentrating on one task and discourage anything that could pose as a distraction. Remember to inject small breaks every hour or so. This is important because when used effectively it helps to freshen the mind and you end up getting back to your task with renewed vigor. It also increases productivity. You will find yourself completing your work in less time, and when you prioritize your most important work in the morning, the rest of the day will seem relatively straightforward.

Priorities in Relationships

Many of us have friendships that we know, but maybe do not always admit, are bad for us. Do not be too concerned; this is usually not a conscious choice! In this instance, we can use self-discipline to identify and prioritize who our true friends are, which can of great benefit in our lives. For example, if you spend time with people who are at all negative toward you or who drain your mental energy through their words and actions, it can serve to reduce the quality time spent with those who are positive elements in your life. Therefore, you need to make decisions. Write down the friends that you have, leaving some space at the side of this list to evaluate those friendships. As an example, have a look at the chart below. This shows you a model of what you need to be taking notice of. The names, in this case, are hypothetical and are simply there as an example to highlight the point.

Friend's name	Positive influence	Negative influence	No influence
Jackie		×	
Ian	×		
Jennifer			×

From the above (and I am sure your list will be longer than this), you can see that the negative influence is Jackie. Why? She demands a lot of attention, and when she visits, she creates the kind of tension that does not make her an overly welcome guest. We all know or have met people like this, whose needs work away at eroding our energy. These are people who may ask a lot of favors or demand a substantial amount of your time, but when you ask them to assist you in any way, usually decline. Now Ian, on the other hand, is a positive influence. If I spend more time with Ian, the chances are that I am going to respond to life in general in a more positive and productive manner. As for Jennifer, she remains neutral and tends not to influence my life in any major way.

When you identify your friends that provide genuine love and support, including family members, you quickly realize who is detrimental to your mental health and those who will help you to become more valuable as a human being. The more time that we spend with people who make us feel wanted and included, the more valuable our life experiences become. We also naturally cultivate the thought that positivity surrounds us. This can be used as an important advantage when it comes to process of self-discipline. For example, imagine the three people in the above scenario ask you to assist them with a task. Jennifer, who lacks direct influence in your life, will be neither here nor there if you accept or decline. Jackie, on the other hand, will potentially take advantage of you by expecting more than is required, while Ian would only ask you to do things he knows you enjoy and would like to do.

Many of us waste too much of our time and energy on negative people. We must identify and make it a habit to consciously spend less time with those who impact our lives in a negative way. It is far better to surround ourselves with people who are positive but also honest and affirming and challenging. It will impact your life in such a positive way that it will make you wonder how you ever managed to function without it. This places you in an environment that means you are more likely to embrace positive and constructive habits. This, in turn, will help incentivize your use of self-discipline more naturally. This is a particularly useful exercise to undertake when you find yourself mentally exhausted.

Prioritizing Your Leisure Time

Now, I want us to examine how much of your leisure time you feel is wasted. There are always certain things we want to undertake or participate in but often convince ourselves that we do not have sufficient time in our lives. Our next example involves looking at the average day for a man called Joe. Joe is, of course, a hypothetical person for example purposes. Joe, like ourselves, has wishes and desires about what he wants to achieve, but he does little to nothing to achieve them.

This is a classic case of creating an environment of self-dissatisfaction, which usually leads to resentment; the byproduct of which can erode the incentive to succeed. Sometimes, if we feel we will never do all the things we want to do, it can be difficult to motivate ourselves to do all the things we are obliged to do. These are the activities you need to monitor in the week ahead.

☐ Watching TV intentionally

☐ Watching TV senselessly

☐ Reading

☐ Doing a hobby

☐ Sports

☐ Learning something new

☐ Eating

☐ Socializing

In Joe's case, he found he was watching senseless television for a large portion of his week. The TV was on making noise in the background, but Joe had no idea of what the program was. He did not read; he did not partake in any hobbies. He did not participate in sports and never really learned anything new. He did, however, socialize at weekends.

When you examine how you utilize your time, you can learn to develop new habits that help you to exercise self-discipline. Learning is one of them. Perhaps you want to learn to play the guitar. Go ahead and learn. Perhaps you have a lot of books to read but never get around to it. Start reading. Perhaps you do not socialize enough. Call a friend and go for a coffee. The point is that you are the only one who can use self-discipline to decide upon your own priorities.

Putting an hour aside to read a book or putting your phone away in the evening so that you can concentrate on enjoying a film, or the company of your friends or family, are all beneficial habits with positive outcomes. Parents should be encouraging a mix of entertainment and educational television programs, rather than sitting their children in front of a television with no structure attached. When you plan and then look forward to a good program, it can increase the value of the program you intend to view. But if it becomes a constant of mindless occupation that gets in the way of your time spent on other more productive aspects, then you need to know when to turn it off or avoid it completely.

When you are effective with the habits that surround your time management, additional time is produced. This will give you all the time you need to enjoy the things that matter to you and enrich your life.

Step Four: Learning to Delegate

So often in our lives we undertake a task because we feel it is easier to do it ourselves rather than delegate it to someone else. It is certainly something I have been guilty of in the past. Saying that, a certain part of this thinking is quite logical. However, there are many things other people can do better than ourselves, and in a far more efficient manner. If you employ the strategy and fail to delegate, you run the risk of compromising the progress of your goals. I have seen this time and time again in a work environment where people regularly try to make themselves indispensable. Unfortunately, in that environment, no one is, and although doing more than expected is an honorable pursuit, it is rarely rewarded. If you practice delegation, however, the set tasks are completed in better time, which, in turn, promotes and solidifies your place in the team. This principle can be applied to your home environment or in your workplace. If you acknowledge that someone can do something better than you, there is strength in asking for their help. This kind of collaboration produces a more productive environment for all involved.

All too often, people can become quite negative because they have assumed too much work or responsibilities. This can easily be avoided if delegated effectively. When you admit that you are struggling and have a problem, it opens the doors to solutions. When at home, do not be afraid to ask for assistance if you feel under pressure. The last thing you or members of your family want is any resentment toward the process or the people in it. It can also serve as a positive message to the younger members of your family as well. By showing that the load can be shared by everyone it promotes inclusion and cooperation.

Chapter Five: Looking After Yourself

"You can't pour from an empty cup. Look after yourself first." - **Anon**

How often do you catch yourself saying you will change one of your habits? At one time or another we are all guilty of it. The irony of that situation is that reciting and internalizing this desire can become a bad habit. Such negative habits will only lead you to a negative place and, in truth, could result in resentment towards yourself.

Step Five: Learning Energy Creates Energy

This is a lesson I believe we all need to learn. When people stop energizing themselves, it is hardly surprising that apathy lies in wait. It is a natural byproduct of a lack of energy. Therefore, giving your body energy needs to take priority, so that it can undertake additional tasks with a decrease in overall effort. Below is a list of issues that may arise if you examine your habits close enough. Some of these may not apply to you, and there may be more that you want to add. It is purely an exercise to guide you on your path to create a list of your own showing the bad habits that take away your energy. Maybe try making a quick note of them now before looking at the following example list.

Habit	Remedy

I do not exercise enough	Do something energetic that you enjoy and that is not a chore. Swimming is good and dancing is fun. You do not have to equate these habits with grueling hard work. A walk around the block can be of great benefit.
I eat too much	Cut out all snacking between meals.
I drink too much	Reduce your quantities so that you drink for pleasure rather than to get drunk.
I procrastinate	Work out one thing you have been putting off and simply act.
I am always telling myself it does not matter.	Everything matters. Make one thing matter today.
I lie on the sofa too much	Switch off the TV and spend an hour in the garden.

When you break down the activities that can actually provide you with more energy, don't feel that you have to undertake all of these at once. Small but decisive steps will improve each of your habits in an effective and applicable manner. Major adjustments tend to be too overwhelming. One method to energize yourself mentally and physically is to create realistic goals and to keep them. Even small goals hold great worth. Each one takes you one step further away from the bad habit that is presenting a negative view of yourself. This, in itself, will provide you with increased energy levels.

If you need the incentive to introduce exercise into your life, there are many steps or methods you can adopt to help you want to get active. If other methods have proven to have little to no effect on your self-motivation, increase your responsibilities to find it. An example of this thinking would be to buy or adopt a dog. They always need walking and will enthusiastically accompany you when you go out. You will also find that you think less of yourself and more of your pet and are thus prone to think of the dog's needs. You may not realize it, but this means in effect that the dog is helping you to help yourself. You will also gain a great friend in your life as a bonus.

The other aspect that requires serious consideration regarding energy levels is sleep. If you do not give yourself sufficient sleep, you are likely to be ineffective, demotivated and stressed. The human need for a certain amount of sleep differs from one individual to another. However, you can average it out at about 7 to 8 hours. If you find that you are not getting enough sleep, then you can use self-discipline to remedy the cause. Make sure that your bed is made as soon as you get up in the morning meaning it is fresh and welcoming at night. The room should be aired regularly and should be conducive to sleep. Do your best to eliminate technology into the bedroom. It can be tempting to watch TV on your iPad or telephone until the twilight hours, which immediately defeats the purpose of the act.

Step Six: Learn to Relax the Mind

There are several ways that you can achieve this. The body scan is a great exercise to help you to get off to sleep at night. Lie on your back and imagine each part of your body, starting with your toes. Then contract and de-contract that part of your body so that it feels totally relaxed. Move to the next part of the body, and so on until you reach the top of your head. This is a proven method to help relax the mind.

For some people, mindfulness helps. What this means is letting go of negative thoughts and feelings and giving yourself time to see things as they really are. When all is said and done, the past is the past and there is not one thing anyone can do to change it. What has happened in the past has gone. What happens in the future will happen regardless of whether you think about it or not, so concentrating your thoughts here – apart from normal forward planning – are wasted. Be in this moment and start to awaken your senses in the now. What does this mean? It means being able to taste, smell, to see, to feel, to touch anything that is relevant to this moment, and nothing else. If any other thoughts enter your mind about any other moment but now, let them go.

Meditation

This is a wonderful habit to embrace. The method was once described to myself as training your mind to reside in the gap between one thought and the next. When studies were done on the brains of monks, scientists were surprised to see differences in the way that their minds worked. They were able to concentrate much more efficiently, and it reshaped and remapped areas of their brain that dealt with basic functions and levels of concentration. To practice meditation, a good start is to set your alarm 20 minutes earlier and take advantage of this time to sit and contemplate the now. Sit on a hard chair with your feet flat on the floor and start to breathe slowly and deeply. Most human beings only use a small capacity of their lung capability, and this technique helps ease and focus the mind. When you meditate, use this deep breathing technique to help the process. The parasympathetic nervous system works better when you do this, which means your body becomes more efficient, and you suffer less stress.

Breathe in through the nostrils to the count of 9. Breathe out to the count of 11. The reason for the differences in the count is that you are trying to normalize the amount of oxygen in the bloodstream. It slows your heart, and it has also shown to cause a small drop in blood pressure. While breathing in this way, place your hand upon your diaphragm, and you will feel the air coming in and the air going out.

Meditation means continuing to do this with your eyes closed and learning to just breathe, uninterrupted by thoughts. When a thought comes into your mind, you acknowledge it and then let it go. Think of it as an intruder. It is not appropriate that it disturbs you right now, so let go of thoughts during the whole meditation process.

It is rather odd that people have the idea that you will feel something, or something is meant to happen right after meditation. Many view it as a quick-fix, which couldn't be further from the truth. In order to unravel the mind, you need to create a habit of meditating daily, and within a couple of weeks, you will find that your thought processes are clearer, your life-goals are clearer, and you begin to feel energized. You may even find that you want to do this several times a day, and it is okay if that is your choice. One word of warning though; it is not a good to practice meditation after you have eaten. The main reason being is that your digestive system will inevitably distract you from your task.

This habit of meditation can be a powerful tool in your self-discipline arsenal. If you have a meeting, for example, you can use a few minutes of meditation before you go in to help your mind to focus on the job at hand. You will also find that it helps you to listen to your body more. When you do that, you can increase your awareness of your body's needs and are more likely to remain healthier for longer.

The times when you can practice meditation are many. Even meditating on the way to work on public transport will helps you to focus on the moment and arrive at work filled with new enthusiasm and energy.

There is a particularly good reason why I included this chapter. Many people are invaded by the world around them. They do not have time to think, or struggle to create the time. The pace of 21st century life is fast, and they are bombarded with alerts in all directions. If you think about it, the 21st-century man is not left to his own devices very often. The phone goes, or someone tells you there is an email. You watch a movie and are invaded by advertisements. The world is a busy place. When you address the balance by using mindfulness and meditation, you change these habits, and you discover that life has so much to offer you. In fact, the Dalai Lama and scientists have recently begun to work together on the topics of depression and anxiety. The symptoms of these in the general population are rife with more and more cases reported every single day. What they have discovered is that there is a link between meditation and the ability to relax. In fact, the discourses between the Dalai Lama and medical experts is actually very well documented if you care to seek out the current information. Countries such as the United Kingdom are now offering anxiety patients courses on mindfulness instead of reverting to regular medications because the long-term effects have been tangible.

I mentioned earlier about self-discipline and meditation helps you to become more self-disciplined. If you use Google, you will find many examples of this and maybe surprised that there are celebrities who use mindfulness and meditation to help them to focus on their successful careers.

Extraordinarily successful people do not just acquire success. They work on it, and one of the best methods of testing your self-discipline is getting up each day and meditating. People such as Oprah Winfrey use meditation to focus on their creative sides so that they can approach life with a different mindset. The one thing that is important about meditation is that thoughts become neutralized. In other words, you learn not to pass judgment on your thoughts, and the way that you feel about your thoughts. When you are able to open your mind to the world around you, discipline becomes easier to live with, and you feel motivated to approach life from a different perspective. You respect people more, and you tend to also generate increased self-respect.

No book on habits and self-discipline would be complete without including the elements of mindfulness and meditation. I would suggest that you try it, and at the end of your morning meditation, keep a note of what you believe you can do next time to make your meditation more effective. For example, if you found that you were in a noisy space, find another space that does not distract you as much. If you could not get rid of thoughts, teach yourself during the day to use mindfulness. Practice being in the moment to help rid yourself of any thoughts that do not pertain to the then and now.

Your mind is what helps you to become a fully-fledged success in life, and any human being who is in good health can use the skills of mindfulness and meditation to enrich themselves. If you have specific problems, you can even throw these into the meditation practice by asking a question before you meditate and then seeing where your meditation takes you.

Meditation also has the benefit of increasing your mobility, your ability to think, and opening the potential to be more open-minded. Open-minded people are usually more self-disciplined than those whose minds are closed to the alternative expression of opinion. This can seriously affect a human being's potential. If you make judgments before looking at problems from all sides, you are shortchanging yourself. Meditation will help you to put this right.

Meditation Instead of Negativity

When you face difficult decisions in your life and want to minimize your maximum risk, meditation will make things clearer to you. Instead of getting into angry retort when you do not agree with someone, you will instead be able to offer alternatives. Your mind will be more versatile, and you will have learned how to use self-discipline to bring out the best in both of you. The intelligent mind always seeks the input of others because when you do, your own picture of success becomes clearer and complete. However, when negativity steps in, encourage others around you to use a positive approach rather than approaching a problem as being something "impossible" to overcome. All things are possible. Surround yourself with people who are open to looking at the problems of life in another way – seeing them as challenges, rather than difficulties. When you turn a difficulty into a challenge, meditation will help your subconscious mind to find solutions.

Chapter Six: 7 Habits of Successful People

We have discussed six of the habit-forming steps that will help take you toward increased success in your life. The habits that have been chosen and highlighted in this chapter dictate how successful you will become when you learn to use self-discipline. You already know the steps that led you here, but you also need to explore these habits because they apply to everyone. Using the criteria shown in the previous chapters, go over the lists that you have made and see whether your conclusions include these habits. If they do not, work your way through them and formulate steps to mirror these guidelines. This will help and guide you on your path to success.

The Habit of Following their Passions

People who are deemed successful are usually so because what they want in life is in line with their passions. They have used their passions to place focus upon what they do with their time, and passion drives them toward success. Self-discipline is also a key component to their success. When you are fueled by passion, what would normally seem like hard work fades into something you are automatically invested in. Successful people push themselves to succeed using their passions as the ultimate motivator.

You can see all kinds of examples of this. Bill Gates is a particularly good example. He believed in his ideas and ideals and started working from a garage. Try to identify what you feel passionate about and see how it could be applied to your life. How can you work toward letting those passions govern your actions? It is extremely hard to become successful if you are in a job that you find difficult to enjoy. However, if you know it is leading you toward your eventual goal, by identifying your passions, you will be able to use self-discipline principles to help you through the difficult days. Just knowing that your determination is leading you somewhere you want to be, then almost anything can be used as a positive stepping-stone, even setbacks.

Passions drive you toward doing difficult things first instead of dreading them and leaving them until last. They help you to define your priorities and give you the drive that you need to use your self-discipline to advantage.

The Habit of Removing Distractions

Earlier in the book, I explained the pathology of distractions and their negative side effects. For example, if you choose to be distracted at bedtime rather than going to sleep, you will lose-out on necessary down-time. In another instant, I explained the importance of job prioritization and avoiding being distracted by your surroundings. If you create this habit, then life becomes a lot easier. Turn off your emails. Put your phone onto voicemail and encourage colleagues to not disturb you while you complete the difficult tasks you have prioritized. The system of working for a set amount of time and then taking breaks refreshes the mind, and you will achieve more. Having achieved your highest priorities, the remainder of your day becomes significantly easier. If you reverse the process and avoid prioritized tasks you will attempt to complete them when your energy is at its lowest, which will be to the detriment of you and your work.

The Habit of Appropriate Reward

What do you achieve by changing your viewpoint? You achieve the ability to use self-discipline to succeed. What is the reward? The ultimate reward is that you succeed. However, if you need small rewards along the way to help motivate the process, then that is more than acceptable. They will help you to get from one stepping-stone to the next in your life. The biggest reward you gain from developing habits like meditation is that you are rewarded with a clear sense of purpose.

The Habit of Doing the Hard Things First

I covered this topic under the heading of prioritization. We have discussed its importance and that you receive a greater sense of achievement if you use your high energy time to action your most difficult of tasks. For some people, the evening is a high energy time. For most, after a good night's sleep, the morning offers this high energy time. But only you can know when your mental energy is at its highest. This is the time that you need to reserve to carry out your most difficult tasks. There are so many tasks that make up a day. If you follow this protocol, it frees up the remainder of your time to undertake the mundane and easy tasks that do not require the same amount of mental energy.

Most people try their best to avoid the difficult tasks they do not want to do. Procrastinators use this strategy all the time. If you have never heard the expression "The road to hell is paved with good intentions," it directly applies to these kinds of people. The way to stop procrastination is to simply begin the task at hand. You can always adapt and tackle smaller tasks if your main task overwhelms you, but do it none the less.

The Habit of Making Decisions

Decision making puts you to the test and exposes your character. Successful people are particularly good at making decisions because they can analyze problems and put together effective remedial action. Through the examination of your thought pattern, as you have throughout this book, you now know that you are more than capable of making decisions. Being indecisive means that doubt yourself and others. It gives the impression that you do not have the confidence needed to make those decisions. However, if you take judgment out of the equation and can address problems taking all perspectives into account, it will reduce the difficulty to make correct decisions.

The Habit of Knowing Yourself and Your Own Biological Clock

When explaining to you how meditation and mindfulness work, and how you acquire such habits, you were given some advice on when best to undertake these things. The reason for this is that different people keep different hours that work for them. Mornings are known as a good time to meditate, but you may find that your biological clock tells you otherwise. If this is the case, choose a time when you can meditate peacefully without upsetting that biological clock. The fact that you commit to a time and perform the task regularly will heighten and strengthen your ability to see the world clearly.

The last habit forms the final step toward using effective self-discipline, before the real journey begins by putting into action what you have learnt here in this book.

Step Seven: Taking Action

'Problems are just opportunities in disguise." – **George Washington**

The most important step of all...

If you have practiced the exercises in this book, you now need to put your learning into action. Whenever you are faced with decision making, as discussed, you need to be able to act. If you are in the habit of out-thinking yourself and using excuses to delay the task, then this is a great opportunity! Let us begin your next journey by welcoming such problems and recognizing them for the great teachers they are.

People who are successful do not just give up when something goes wrong. They use their mistakes as a learning platform to help inspire them on to their next effort. Self-discipline means an examination of why something did not work and being able to try and try again until it does. Mistakes are opportunities. They teach you so much about why things do not work, which can be of more value than understanding the things that do. If you see them in a positive light and as an opportunity rather than a barrier, you begin to actually look forward to the next hurdle, knowing that what you have learned will ensure that your next attempt at action is a success.

Conclusion

There is a lot of information packed into the pages of this book, and this is just the beginning. You now know what self-discipline is and how to apply it in your life. However, until you act, you will not begin to see the change you are seeking in yourself. I suggest that you take some time to go back over the exercises and examine your own barriers to entry. We all have them, but when you appraise them, you learn more about yourself and your own methodology. Each person is an individual, which is why the exercises are individual exercises and require your focus and input.

I would also suggest that you test the waters and try to change a few small habits to begin with, keeping in mind that the brain takes about 40 days to grasp a new habit. I explained to you how you can cheat a little and utilize leapfrogging habits. I have also taught you how to assess your own weaknesses and the weaknesses in the way you think. People around you will also have an influence on your mindset. Only you can change these approaches, and you now have all the material you need to get started within the pages of this book.

One thing I am quite confident of is that if you choose to explore mindfulness and meditation, your views of yourself will almost certainly begin to change. The reason may not be obvious at the beginning of your journey into this area of your life, but these techniques can be used as powerful tools to help recognize your key values and act as a signposts on the road of life. Sometimes we find that too much choice, or too many forms of advice on one subject, can overwhelm the mind with unlimited ideas and ideals. Meditation gets you closer to the authentic you so that all this outside influence does not alter your true perspective. You can begin to appreciate your passions and use them to drive you forward. You will also learn not to judge your thoughts, but merely to observe them and extract from them what is useful in your life – rather than having your life dictated by the negativity of your thoughts.

I wish you well on your journey and know that you have self-discipline within your capabilities. We all do. It is just a case of prioritizing, choosing our friendships well, and learning to approach life with a positive mindset while embracing the lessons negativity can teach. Once you achieve that, your life will change for the better using self-discipline as a steadfast guide. The world is waiting for you. Now is time to work toward turning your dreams into reality. Now, get to work!

www.ingramcontent.com/pod-product-compliance
Lightning Source LLC
Chambersburg PA
CBHW071253130726
47998CB00003B/1170